The Miracle of

written by Amy B. Pedersen

designed by Betty Hood

Published by Marian Press
Stockbridge, MA 01263
1-800-462-7426
www.marian.org

www.amypedersen.com

International Standard Book Number: 978-1-59872-738-8

Dedication

To God, thank You … for everything.

To my amazing husband, Jon, and
our two precious miracles,
I love you "the whole world much!"

Acknowledgements

With sincere gratitude, I would like to thank:

Betty Hood, owner of JBH Designs, for her countless hours of design and layout assistance and her unwavering commitment and encouragement for this project. We've come a long way, Baby!

Dr. Gerry Sotomayor, founder of Babies for Life Foundation, for his guidance and enthusiasm for the book.

Fr. Frank Pavone, Priests for Life, and the Seminarian Life Link for donating much of this life-altering photography.

The religious and lay leaders at St. Ann's, especially Fr. Tom Reilly, Rusty Mawn, and Elizabeth Daugherty.

And all my friends and family, especially my Mom, Ree "B" Blankenship, who embraced this effort and shared my passion for this project from day one. I love you.

Go through these pages one by one
and learn a thing or two
about how I will grow each week
while I'm in this precious womb.

The pictures you will see
are those of babies on the way.
I thought you'd like to visualize
how I look on different days.

Although I'll grow and grow
at my own unique pace,
the other pictures represent
average babies' heights and weights.

Things will certainly be different soon,
no doubt you know that's true.
Know that I'm a miracle of life,
God's special gift to YOU.

I love you!

Week 1

God is getting things ready.
The time is almost here.
Although you may be nervous,
there's nothing you should fear.

Week

I'll be such a blessing,
just you wait and see.
I'm a miracle of life —
a gift from God — that's me!

● ● ● ● ● ● ● ● ●

Week

Now inside Mommy's body,
I'm a teeny tiny cell.
Although I'm itty bitty,
I'm already doing well.

9

Week 4

I'm growing in a sac
where for several weeks and days,
I'll sleep and eat and grow
in very special ways.

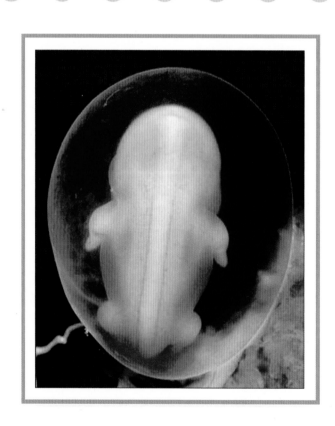

Day 28

Week 5

God's plans are all in place,
and I'm really growing fast.
Mommy may not be feeling well
but you know this will not last.

Week 6

My facial features start to form,
and dimples mark my ears.
Tiny buds will be my arms and legs.
A beating heart appears.

Week

I'm really growing quickly,
although I'm still quite small.
I'm heavy as an eyelash
and now one-third inch tall.

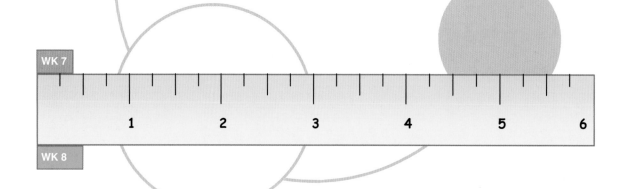

WK 7

1   2   3   4   5   6

WK 8

Week

I'm already nearing one-half inch,
twice as big as eight days ago.
My arms and legs are in proportion
with lots more growing to go.

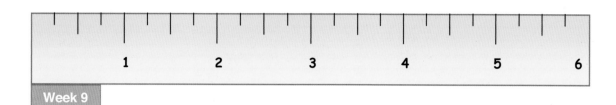

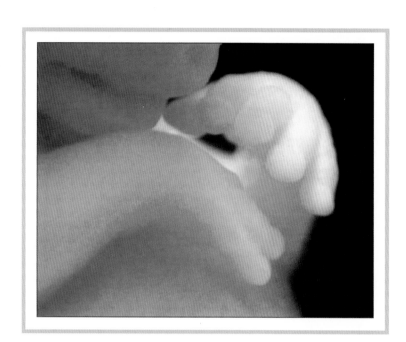

Week 9

My brain is sending signals
to my muscles so I can move.
My fingers and my thumbs appear,
and I continue to improve.

Week 10

My taste buds begin to develop,
and my arms bend at the elbow.
My tongue and ears are formed.
Just seven more months to go!

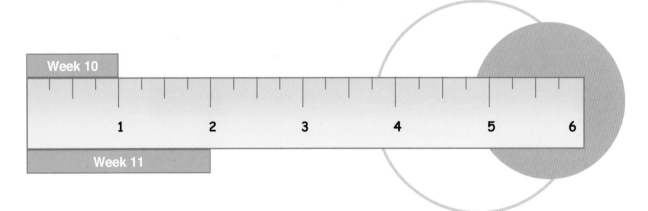

Week 10

| 1 | 2 | 3 | 4 | 5 | 6 |

Week 11

Week 11

In one week's time, I'm twice as big
to roughly two inches tall.
Fingernails and toenails begin to grow,
though they're very, very, small.

Week 12

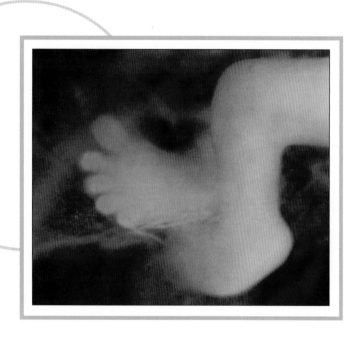

1/2 oz

I love my brand new reflex.

My mouth opens when I touch my face.

And in only seven short days,

my weight doubled within this space.

Week  13

All 20 teeth have grown in my gums,

and vocal chords are formed in their box.

But sounds do not travel through fluid.

They fly through the air like birds in their flocks.

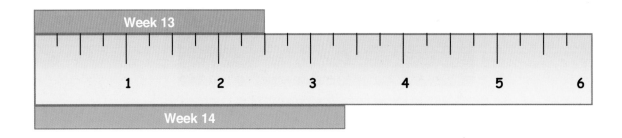

Week 13

Week 14

1   2   3   4   5   6

Week 14

I'm a very active baby

with much to do and to explore.

I practice inhaling and exhaling

and wiggling my fingers more and more.

Week

Using a special machine,
the doctor hears my heart beat.
I move more now, and I enjoy
making fists and wiggling my feet.

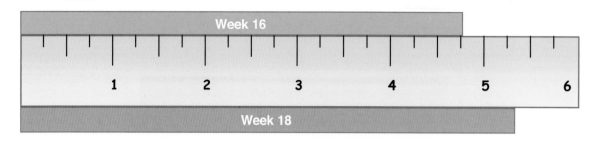

Week 16

Week 18

Week 16

During this exciting fourth month,

my body grows faster than my head.

I can now hold my head upright.

Each toenail grows from its nail bed.

Week

I am working really hard now
to grow to be like you.
I'm blinking, sucking, and swallowing,
just to name a few.

Week 18

The pads on my fingers and toes
are blank for God to tweak.
He'll add swirls and lines and other designs
so I will be unique.

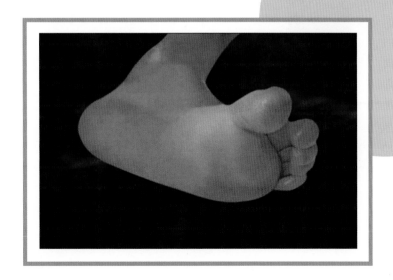

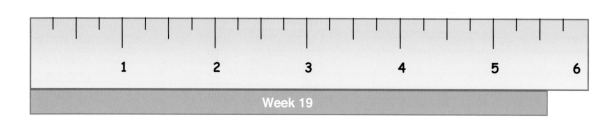

Week 19

Mommy's been pregnant for four months now.
She is almost half way there.
This month, I'll add an extra pound and a half
and another two inches to spare.

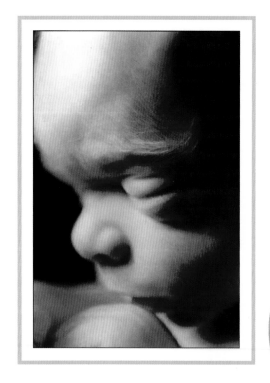

Week 20

Fine hair is starting to grow.
My eyebrows are beginning to form.
I snuggle up in my favorite position
and I sleep as much as a newborn.

20

Week

I bend and stretch and I bump Mommy's tummy,

and I am already very smart.

I look like a small newborn, and I'm stronger now,

especially my muscles, bones, and heart.

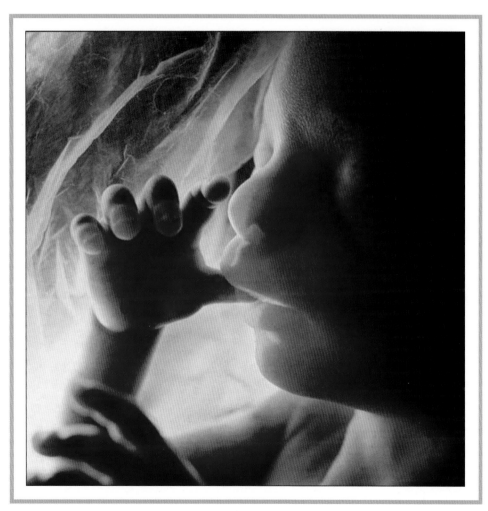

1   2   3   4   5   6   7

Week 21

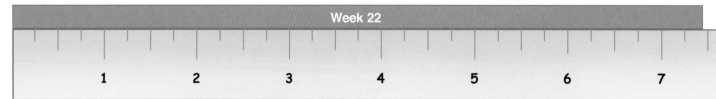

Week

My eyebrows and head hair can be seen,

and my hands can make quite a grip.

My brain grows quickly from now 'til I'm five

when I will run, skip, jump and flip.

Week  23

Four weeks from now I will weigh
twice as much as I do today.
Mommy can really feel me move
since my arms and legs like to play.

● ● ● ● ● ● ● ● ●

Week 24

Every day, I hear sounds
that my Mommy's body makes.
Her beating heart, her pretty voice,
and every breath she takes.

1.3 lbs

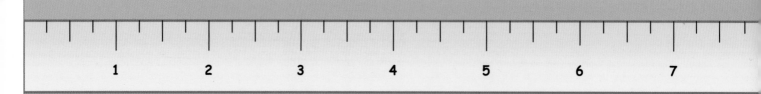

Week 25

Underneath my supple skin,
tiny blood vessels grow.
As blood flows through my body,
my skin has a soft pink glow.

Week 26

My senses are developing
as I practice looking and hearing each day.
At roughly nine inches long and almost two pounds,
there is less room for me to play.

2 lbs.

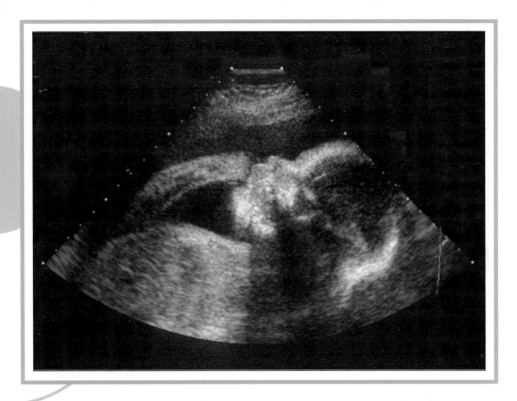

Look! I'm sucking my thumb!

Week 2 7

This week I will grow
roughly one-half an inch more.
My brain wave patterns are like those
of a baby who's just been born.

25

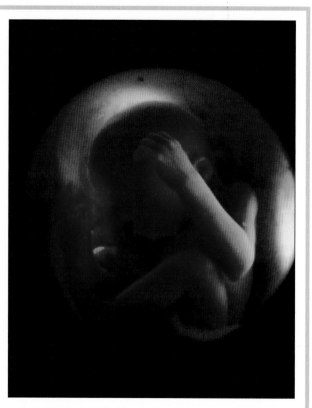

Week 28

My eyes are now able to open.
But even better than that,
my lungs can breathe air like yours do.
Now what do you think of that?

26

9   10   11   12   13   14   15   16

Week 2 9

This week, I'm becoming more sensitive
to light, sound, taste, and smell.
My brain can direct my breathing
and my temperature as well.

Week 3 0

By now God may have topped me
with one lovely head of hair.
I am His beautiful creation.
When I'm born, you'll want to stare!

27

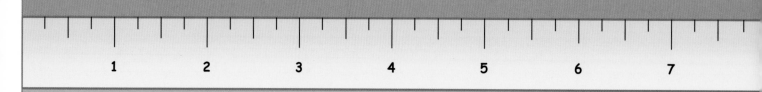

Week  3 1

It is really getting tight in here.

There's less room to move around.

I tuck my legs up to my chest.

I'm ten inches from rump to crown.

Week 3 2

I am now in touch with my senses.

When responding to a light,

I'll gently close my eyes

if I think it's much too bright.

28

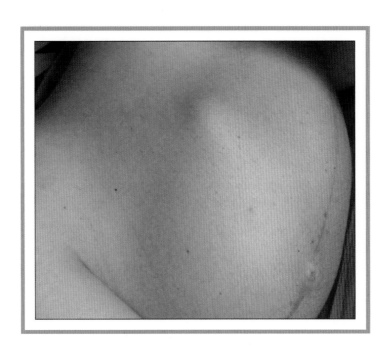

That's me kicking!

Week 33

My head keeps getting bigger
to make room for my growing brain.
I suck on my thumb or my fingers,
and weight I continue to gain.

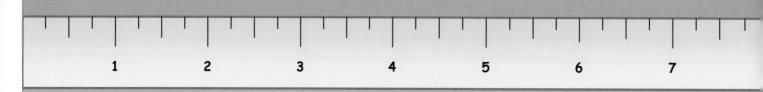

Week

Inside, my eyes are open
when I'm awake and I'm alert.
Outside, Mommy's tummy keeps growing
so she wears bigger pants and shirts.

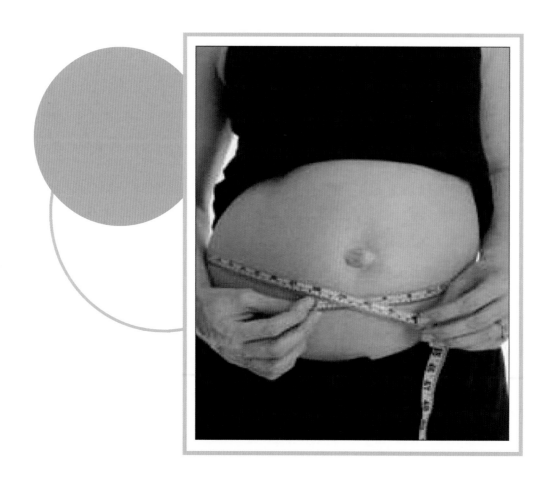

Week 35

I'm at least four and a half pounds
and roughly 12 inches long this week.
My arms and legs are getting chubby,
just like my little round cheeks!

Week 36

Growth has finally slowed down
to save energy for when I'm born.
Some body fat is being stored
so when it's time, I can keep warm.

Week

Most babies are born within two weeks
of their doctor's forecasted due date.
Only God knows when I will arrive though.
There is not too much longer to wait!

Week

My arms and legs are tucked close to my body
since there is not much room to spare.
I can't wait to meet you and to learn from you,
like how to play, to walk, and to share.

32

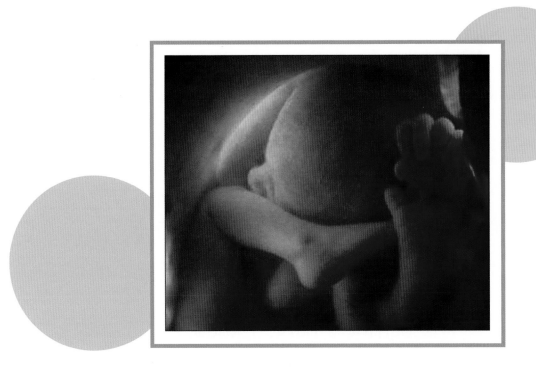

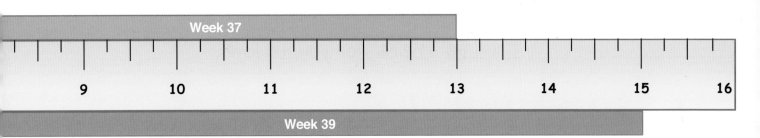

Week 37

9 10 11 12 13 14 15 16

Week 39

Week  39

My skin becomes thicker and paler,
and dimples and creases appear.
One half ounce of fat is stored each day
as my own birthday draws near.

7 lbs.

Week  4 0

The time is getting closer.

I am ready for my debut.

My head is soft to ease the birth.

Soon, I'll be there to meet you!

The waiting is hard, I know.

God will send you strength from above.

And just when you think you can't wait anymore,

I will be there for you to love.

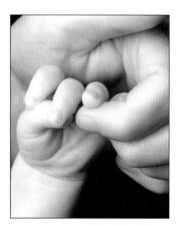  

34

And now a
New Chapter
Begins . . .

A Note from the Author

The news of a baby on the way can bring a range of emotions. For some, immense joy and happiness. For others, well … not so much. As the oldest of four children, I can remember the excitement I felt when I learned that Mom was pregnant with "the baby". As the only girl to date in the line-up, I *knew* that God had little pink dresses and hair bows in our future. There was no doubt in my mind. Imagine my surprise when the baby was born and I learned that he was a boy! Shock and disbelief were an understatement. I am 99 percent certain that I screamed at the news. I certainly did in my head. It just couldn't be true. Three boys and one girl? *There was absolutely no way!*

This anxiety and, frankly, anger was replaced with love and affection for this precious child as soon as I met him. He melted me to the core. And every preconceived notion I had about my awful reality disappeared when I held him for the first time. I learned a very important lesson that day. It was not only about me!!! God's plans for this boy were much bigger than my desires to have someone to paint toe nails with. This really had very little to do with me. I was just an instrument in his growth and development. God had a much bigger mission in store for my baby brother.

Fast forward about twenty years. This time I was the pregnant one and expecting my first child. Again, I felt a range of emotions but it was different, for sure … Much different. I was hesitant but excited. Nervous but optimistic. Scared yet amazed. At the end of my emotional roller coaster though, it was clear to me that Jon and I were chosen to be this precious baby's parents. We were chosen to raise this child. After all, God had a great plan for this child (and *every* child), and we were simply vessels in making this happen.

To this day, I'm filled with wonder. I am amazed that we were entrusted with this awesome responsibility and even more amazed that we've been able to pull it off (with God's help, of course). Despite our initial uncertainties about parenthood, we've done alright. In fact, we're proud that both of our children have done so well so far. We're raising these beautiful little people to fulfill God's plan. Not only the plans He has for them, but the plans He has for us. Each life is precious and a gift from God. After all, we are all chosen by Him.

You Were Chosen

John 15:16

"You did not choose Me but I chose you. And I appointed you to go and bear fruit, fruit that will last, so that the Father will give you whatever you ask him in My name."

Jeremiah 1:5

"Before I formed you in the womb I knew you."

Jeremiah 28:11

"For surely I know the plans I have for you, says the Lord, plans for your welfare and not for harm, to give you a future with hope."

About the Author

Amy B. Pedersen received a Bachelor's degree in Journalism from The University of Georgia and a Master's degree in Marketing from Georgia State University. She has worked at several advertising and promotional agencies in Atlanta. She is an active member and volunteer of St. Ann's Catholic Church in Marietta, Georgia. She has been married to Jonathan Pedersen for eleven years and they are the proud parents of their own two young miracles. www.amypedersen.com

About the Designer

Betty Hood is the owner of JBH Designs, a print and web firm in Canton, Georgia. She has 16 years experience with a major Fortune 500 company in information technology as well as training and development. Betty is enrolled in the University of the South's four-year Education for Ministry Training Program for lay ministry. She is an active parishioner and volunteer at St Aidan's Episcopal Church in Alpharetta, Georgia. Married to Jerry Hood, she is the proud mother of two adult children and the loving "Nana" of five grandchildren. www.jbhdesigns.com

Photography Credits